Oct 2014

First Facts®

Birds

Vultures

by Cecilia Pinto McCarthy

Consultant:
Tanya Dewey, PhD
University of Michigan Museum of Zoology
Ann Arbor, Michigan

CAPSTONE PRESS
a capstone imprint

First Facts is published by Capstone Press,
1710 Roe Crest Drive, North Mankato, Minnesota 56003.
www.capstonepub.com

Library of Congress Cataloging-in-Publication Data
McCarthy, Cecilia Pinto.
 Vultures / by Cecilia Pinto McCarthy.
  p. cm.—(First facts. birds)
 Includes bibliographical references and index.
 Summary: "Discusses vultures, including their physical features, habitat,
range, and life cycle"—Provided by publisher.
 ISBN 978-1-4296-8608-2 (library binding)
 ISBN 978-1-62065-254-1 (ebook PDF)
 1. Vultures—Juvenile literature. I. Title.

 QL696.F32M336 2013
 598.9'2—dc23
                              2012002142

Editorial Credits:
Lori Shores, editor; Juliette Peters, designer; Kathy McColley, production specialist

Photo Credits:
Alamy: A & J Visage, 20, blickwinkel/Schmidbauer, 7, Premaphotos, 5; Corbis: Visuals
Unlimited/Tom Ulrich, 19; Newscom: KRT/Rick Martin, 11, Photoshot/Evolve/Nigel
J Dennis, 14, Splash News/Solent News, 21, Visual & Written, 6; Shutterstock: Evgeniy
Ayupov, cover, John A. Anderson, 13, Nick Biemans, 8, palko72, 17, Peter Wollinga, 1

Artistic Effects
Shutterstock: ethylalkohol, Pavel K, pinare

Essential content terms are **bold** and are defined at the bottom of the page where they
first appear.

Printed in the United States of America in North Mankato, Minnesota.

042012   006682CGF12

Table of Contents

The Clean Team 4

Vulture Bodies 6

Keeping Clean 9

Where Vultures Live 10

New World Vultures 12

Old World Vultures 15

A Strong Stomach 16

A Vulture's Life 18

Growing Up 20

Amazing but True! 21

Glossary 22

Read More 23

Internet Sites 23

Index 24

The Clean Team

A vulture spots a dead animal from high in the sky. The huge bird lands and tears at the body with a sharp, hooked beak. Soon more **scavengers** arrive. Within hours, only bones are left. Large vultures can eat 2 to 3 pounds (0.9 to 1.4 kilograms) of meat at one meal.

Vulture Fact!

Vultures are nature's cleaners. They get rid of dead bodies that may spread disease.

scavenger—an animal that eats dead animals

wings

eyes

beak

talons

African white-backed vultures

Vulture Bodies

Vultures come in all sizes. The largest are Andean condors weighing up to 33 pounds (15 kg). Egyptian vultures are only the size of chickens.

Egyptian vulture

Andean condor

Strong, broad wings help vultures **soar**. These powerful fliers can travel for hours without tiring.

king vulture

Keeping Clean

Vultures are not flashy birds. They have brown or black feathers and bare heads. Their bald heads stay clean while feasting inside **carcasses**.

Unlike most vultures, the king vulture is colorful. Its body is black and white. The skin on its head is red, orange, and yellow.

Vulture Fact!

Bare skin also helps vultures shed body heat to keep cool.

carcass—the body of a dead animal

Where Vultures Live

Different kinds of vultures live throughout most of the world. They live in grasslands, forests, and even in cities. Vultures can live almost anywhere they can find food.

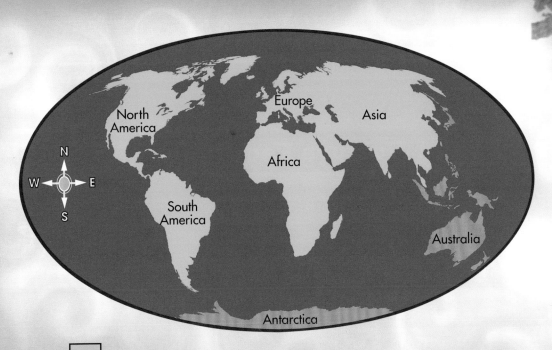

where vultures live

California condor

In 1987 only 22 California condors were left in the world. Wildlife groups rounded up the large birds. By breeding them at zoos, they were able to save them. Today there are more than 350 California condors alive.

New World Vultures

Vultures are divided into two groups. New World and Old World vultures look alike, but are not closely related. Some New World vultures have a good sense of smell to find food. They don't have a **voice box** so they only hiss and grunt. They cannot grab things with their weak feet.

Vulture Fact!

A good sense of smell is unusual in birds. But turkey vultures can smell food from a distance. Other vultures follow turkey vultures to find food.

voice box—a part of the throat that allows an animal to make sound

black vulture

lammergeier vulture

Old World Vultures

Old World vultures are closely related to hawks and eagles. They can make many sounds. Their strong feet have long, grasping **talons**. Old World vultures use their good eyesight to spot dead animals far away.

talon—a large, sharp claw

A Strong Stomach

Vultures eat freshly dead animals. They also eat animals that have begun to rot. Vultures don't get sick from the germs in rotten meat like other animals do. They may kill weak animals for food too. Some vultures also eat fruit, nuts, insects, and fish.

Vulture Fact!

Egyptian vultures eat ostrich eggs that they crack with rocks. This skill makes them one of the few birds to use tools.

Eurasian griffon

A Vulture's Life

New World vultures lay eggs in tree hollows or on cliff ledges and old buildings. Old World vultures make nests in trees or on rocky ledges. Females lay one to three eggs. In 32 to 68 days, the eggs **hatch**.

Vulture Fact!

Before nesting male and female vultures do a sort of dance. They fly and swoop together through the sky.

hatch—to break out of an egg

Life Cycle of a Vulture

Newborn: Chicks break out of shells with a beak part called an egg tooth.

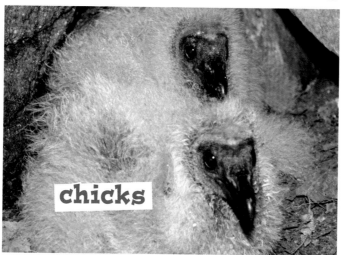

chicks

Young: It may take two years for young vultures to grow all their adult feathers.

Adult: Most vultures live 25 to 30 years. Some can live to be 70 years old.

Growing Up

Newborn chicks are covered in **down**. In three to six months, the chicks will have flying feathers. Some chicks stay near their parents for several years.

Eurasian griffon

Vulture Fact!
Vulture nests stink. The awful smell keeps other animals away.

down—soft, fluffy feathers

Amazing but True!

Some vultures have a gross way of defending themselves. They throw up! The smelly vomit scares away most attackers. But sometimes the attacker sticks around to eat chunks of meat in the vomit. While it's busy eating, the vulture makes its getaway.

Glossary

carcass (KAR-kuhss)—the body of a dead animal

down (DOUN)—soft, fluffy feathers of a bird

hatch (HACH)—to break out of an egg

scavenger (SKAV-uhn-jer)—an animal that feeds on animals that are already dead

soar (SOR)—to fly without flapping wings

talon (TAL-uhn)—a large, sharp claw

voice box (VOISS BOKS)—a part of the throat that allows an animal to make sound

Read More

Lundgren, Julie K. *Vultures*. Raptors. Vero Beach, Fla.: Rourke Pub., 2010.

Macken, JoAnn Early. *Vultures*. Animals That Live in the Desert. Pleasantville, N.Y.: Weekly Reader, 2010.

Magellan, Marta. *Those Voracious Vultures*. Sarasota, Fla.: Pineapple Press, 2008.

Internet Sites

FactHound offers a safe, fun way to find Internet sites related to this book. All of the sites on FactHound have been researched by our staff.

Here's all you do:

Visit *www.facthound.com*

Type in this code: 9781429686082

Super-cool stuff!

Check out projects, games and lots more at
www.capstonekids.com

Index

beaks, 4

chicks, 19, 20
colors, 9

defenses, 21

eating, 4, 9, 16
eggs, 18
egg teeth, 19
eyesight, 15

feathers, 9, 19, 20
feet, 12, 15
food, 4, 10, 12, 16

habitats, 10
hatching, 18, 19
heads, 9

kinds of vultures, 10
  Andean condors, 6, 7
  California condors, 11
  Egyptian vultures, 6, 16
  king vultures, 9
  New World vultures, 12, 18
  Old World vultures, 12, 15, 18
  turkey vultures, 12

life cycle, 19

nests, 18, 20

range, 10

size, 4, 6, 7
soaring, 7

talons, 15

wings, 7